Dr. Wayne W. Dyer
with Kristina Tracy

NO EXCUSES!

HOW WHAT YOU SAY CAN GET IN YOUR WAY

Illustrated by
Stacy Heller Budnick

HAY
HOUSE

HAY HOUSE, INC.
Carlsbad, California • New York City
London • Sydney • Johannesburg
Vancouver • Hong Kong • New Delhi

Copyright © 2009 by Wayne W. Dyer

Published and distributed in the United States by: Hay House, Inc.:
www.hayhouse.com • *Published and distributed in Australia by:* Hay House Australia
Pty. Ltd.: www.hayhouse.com.au • *Published and distributed in the United Kingdom by:*
Hay House UK, Ltd.: www.hayhouse.co.uk • *Published and distributed in the Republic of South
Africa by:* Hay House SA (Pty), Ltd.: www.hayhouse.co.za • *Distributed in Canada by:* Raincoast Books:
www.raincoast.com • *Published in India by:* Hay House Publishers India: www.hayhouse.co.in

Design and Editorial Assistance: Jenny Richards • *Illustrations:* © Stacy Heller Budnick

Library of Congress Control Number: 2009921726

ISBN: 978-1-4019-2583-3

16 15 14 13 12 11 10 9 8
1st edition, June 2009

Printed in the United States of America

Dear Parents and Teachers,

Recently I wrote a book for adults called *Excuses Begone!* It teaches how people can achieve what they desire in life by letting go of the excuses they make once and for all. Wouldn't it be great if children could learn at an early age how to eliminate excuses from *their* lives?

Once your children see how often they use excuses and how excuses stop them from reaching their goals, they can start to change these habits and be free from self-limiting thoughts.

In this book, your child will learn:

- Where excuses come from

- Why people make excuses

- How to stop making excuses

It is my hope that both you and your child will gain insights from these pages, enjoy learning together, and live a life of NO EXCUSES!

Sincerely,

Wayne W. Dyer

Ever since I was born, I have loved **SEA TURTLES**.

I drove my family crazy!

Everyone wondered why I loved sea turtles so much when I lived on a farm. They asked,

"Why not cows?"

"Why not pigs?"

"Why not chickens?"

All these animals are great, but it was sea turtles that I loved, and I was determined to see a real live one.

Here I am on my first trip to the aquarium!

Boy, did I learn a lot that day! Not only did I see my first live sea turtle, but I found out that they are an **ENDANGERED SPECIES!**

They need our help if they are going to survive!

CITY AQUARIUM
ENDANGERED SPECIES

I decided right then and there to devote my life to sea turtles. And I met the perfect person to help me: Dr. Tortuga.

Dr. Tortuga is a scientist, a marine biologist. She is an expert on sea turtles, and her job is to study and protect them.

I wanted to be just like her. I started visiting her whenever I could.

I was very excited. I told everyone that I was going to be a marine biologist and save the sea turtles!

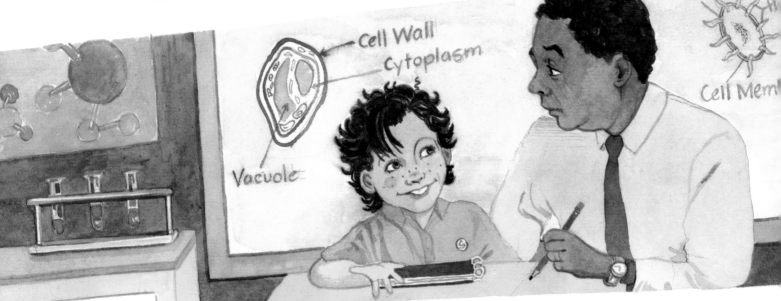

My teacher said, "Wow, you have to be pretty SMART to do that! Science doesn't really seem like your best subject. . . ."

The lady at the shoe store said, "That will take a LONG TIME! Are you sure you want to study that much?"

Mom told me, "You know, we might not have the money to send you to college. If this is something you want, you may need to do it **ON YOUR OWN.**"

Grandpa said, "We are a family of farmers and that is what we have always been. Your dad sure would be **DISAPPOINTED**."

Soon, I started thinking that becoming a marine biologist wasn't such a good idea.

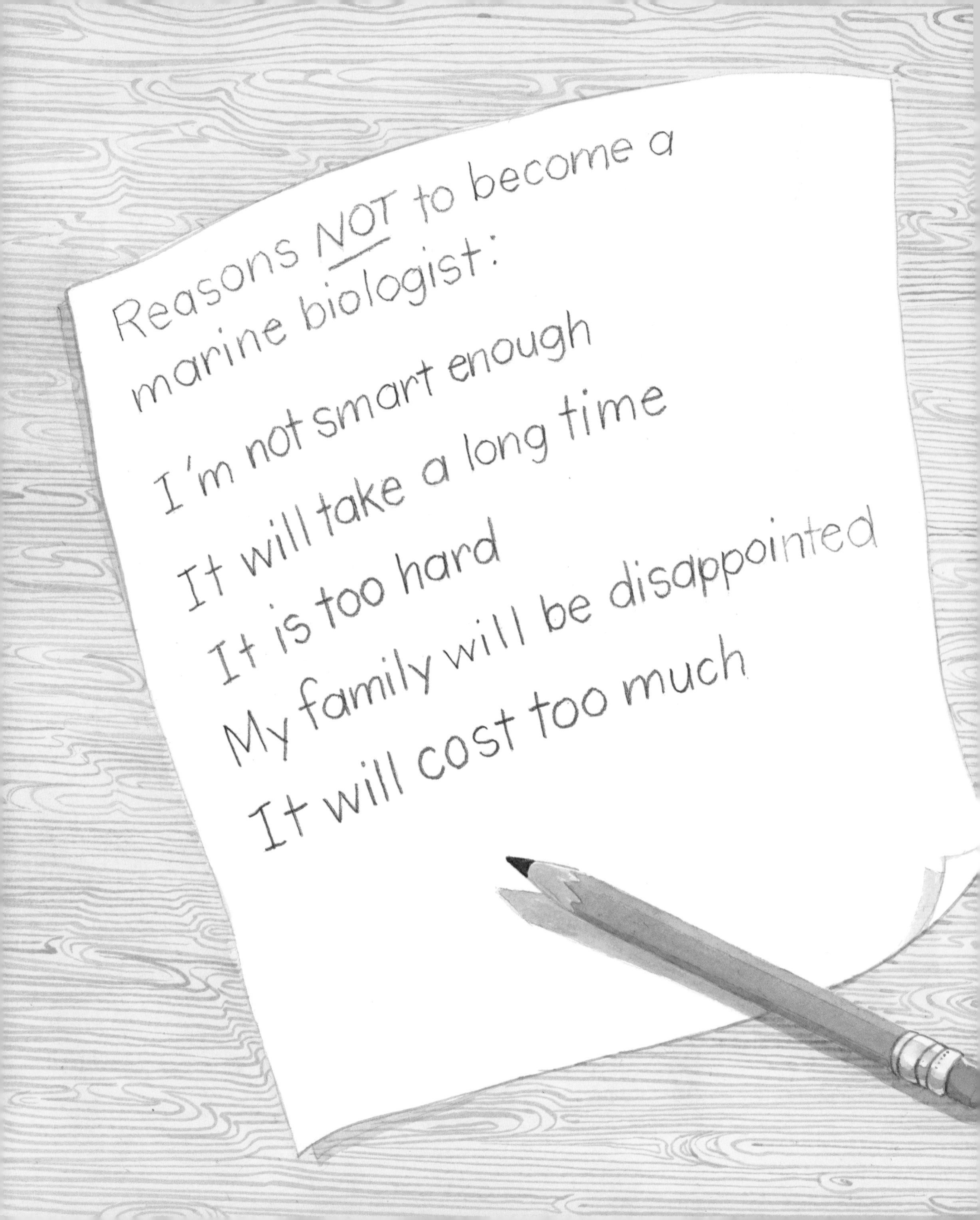

Reasons _NOT_ to become a marine biologist:

I'm not smart enough

It will take a long time

It is too hard

My family will be disappointed

It will cost too much

went to visit Dr. Tortuga at the aquarium. I told her that I wouldn't be coming by anymore. I showed her my list.

"Well," she said, "this is nothing but a list of excuses! Excuses are just words that stop you from doing what you want, being what you want, and having what you want."

"For example, you want to be a marine biologist. You've heard lots of opinions from people, and now you feel like there are things standing in the way of your goal. When you find yourself with a list of excuses like this, it's time to ask yourself some important questions."

WHY AM I MAKING AN EXCUSE?

"People make excuses for all kinds of things. Excuses give us a reason not to do things that seem hard or scary. Making excuses can cause you to miss out on a lot in life!"

WHERE DID THE EXCUSE COME FROM?

"You might want to blame excuses on your parents, teachers, and friends. But no matter what anyone else says, there is only one person an excuse comes from, and that is you. Why? Because only *you* can choose to use the excuse or not."

IS THE EXCUSE TRUE?

"When you say something like, 'It is too hard . . .' to become a marine biologist, or 'My family will be disappointed,' do you know these things are true? Are you 100 percent sure that it will be hard? . . . That people will be disappointed? Of course you don't! The only way you will know is to do it and find out for yourself."

HOW CAN I GET RID OF EXCUSES?

"Now you know where excuses come from, why you make them, and how to find out if they are true. This way you can spot an excuse the minute it comes up and use what you've learned to stop the excuse in its tracks!"

"To make or not make excuses is a choice you have every day. Now here is another choice: you can throw away this list and make a promise to yourself that you will not let excuses get in your way. Without excuses, you are free to be anything you want to be!"

When I went to bed that night, I thought of everything Dr. Tortuga had said. As I slept, I dreamed I was swimming with a giant sea turtle. A whole school of baby turtles swam behind me, and I was surrounded by all the beautiful creatures of the sea.

It was the best feeling ever!

When I woke up, I knew that being a marine biologist was the one thing I wanted to do more than anything in the world and that I would not let excuses get in the way!

I got up and made a new list.

NO MORE EXCUSES!

I am smart

It doesn't matter how long it takes

I will find a way to pay for college

I am not afraid to take a chance

I kept this list and read it every day.

When I was doing homework
and taking tests, I told myself, **"I AM SMART,"** and I believed it.

When I was working in the snack bar, cleaning windows, and caring
for dolphins to earn money for college, I reminded myself that I was
doing this to make my **DREAM COME TRUE.**

Here is a picture of me on the day I left for college.
I was so proud of myself when I got on that train!

Now I am grown up, and I work with sea turtles in Hawaii. I'm sure glad I did not let a bunch of excuses stand in my way!

You have learned that the best way to stop making excuses is to notice when you are making one. Then you can choose to change the excuse to something positive. On these two pages, some of the sentences are excuses and some are not. Have a grown-up read them out loud, and then you can decide if it sounds like an excuse. (If you want, practice turning the excuses into positive words!)

	EXCUSE	NOT AN EXCUSE
I don't want to go ice-skating because I don't know how to do it and I might get hurt.	☐	☐
I'm not good at spelling—nobody in my family is.	☐	☐
I want a new video game, so I am going to walk my neighbor's dog to earn money.	☐	☐
I love basketball, but my cousin said I'm not tall enough to play.	☐	☐
I want to sing in the talent show, but nobody else in my class is doing it.	☐	☐

	EXCUSE	NOT AN EXCUSE
Some people tell me I'm shy, but I know I will make friends at my new school.	☐	☐
This book looks tough, but I know I am smart enough to read it, even if it takes a long time.	☐	☐
I'm not going to the slumber party because I've never slept away from home.	☐	☐
All my sisters do gymnastics, but I am going to try tap dancing!	☐	☐
I really want a skateboard, but it costs too much.	☐	☐
I'm the youngest kid to try out for the chess club, but I'm not going to let that stop me!	☐	☐
Digging a big hole is hard, but I really want to plant this tree, so I'd better get to work.	☐	☐

We hope you enjoyed this Hay House book.
If you'd like to receive our online catalog featuring additional
information on Hay House books and products, or if you'd like
to find out more about the Hay Foundation, please contact:

Hay House, Inc.
P.O. Box 5100
Carlsbad, CA 92018-5100

(760) 431-7695 or (800) 654-5126
(760) 431-6948 (fax) or (800) 650-5115 (fax)
www.hayhouse.com® • www.hayfoundation.org

Published and distributed in Australia by: Hay House Australia Pty. Ltd., 18/36 Ralph St., Alexandria NSW 2015 • Phone: 612-9669-4299
Fax: 612-9669-4144 • www.hayhouse.com.au

Published and distributed in the United Kingdom by: Hay House UK, Ltd., Astley House, 33 Notting Hill Gate, London W11 3JQ
Phone: 44-20-3675-2450 • Fax: 44-20-3675-245 • www.hayhouse.co.uk

Published and distributed in the Republic of South Africa by: Hay House SA (Pty), Ltd., P.O. Box 990, Witkoppen 2068
Phone/Fax: 27-11-467-8904 • info@hayhouse.co.za • www.hayhouse.co.za

Published in India by: Hay House Publishers India, Muskaan Complex, Plot No. 3, B-2, Vasant Kunj, New Delhi 110 070
Phone: 91-11-4176-1620 • Fax: 91-11-4176-1630 • www.hayhouse.co.in

Distributed in Canada by: Raincoast Books, 2440 Viking Way,
Richmond, B.C. V6V 1N2 • Phone: 1-800-663-5714
Fax: 1-800-565-3770 • www.raincoast.com

Take Your Soul on a Vacation

Visit www.HealYourLife.com® to regroup, recharge, and reconnect
with your own magnificence. Featuring blogs, mind-body-spirit news,
and life-changing wisdom from Louise Hay and friends.

Visit www.HealYourLife.com today!